TOM TOPP

and the

GREAT ADVENTURE SWAP

T0342971

Lisa Limbrick

Illustrated by Jemima Trappel

Tom Topp and the Great Adventure Swap

Text © Lisa Limbrick
Illustrations © Jemima Trappel

Published by Wombat Books 2016
www.wombatbooks.com.au
PO Box 1519,
Capalaba QLD 4157
Australia

National Library of Australia Cataloguing-in-Publication entry
Creator: Limbrick, Lisa, author.

Title: Tom Topp and the great adventure swap / Lisa Limbrick ;
 illustrated by Jemima Trappel.
ISBN: 9781925139754 (paperback)
Target Audience: For primary school age.
Subjects: Adventure stories.
 Children's stories.
Other Creators/Contributors: Trappel, Jemima, illustrator.
Dewey Number: A823.4

To my wonderfully supportive husband and inspiring children, thank you for always believing in me
- LL

Chapter 1

Tom stared at the plaster cast. It looked like a giant white cocoon wrapped around his leg. He tried to wedge his finger under the plaster to scratch his leg but it wouldn't budge. The cocoon held on like it was strapped to a supersonic rocket.

Instead, Tom tried to move his leg into a more comfortable position but he could barely get it off the lounge.

The hugely uncomfortable LUMPY lounge.

'Hey Henry,' said Tom to one of his older brothers, 'chuck me a cushion.'

'Sure, dude,' said Henry, and hurled Mum's favourite pink flamingo cushion at him.

'Hey, watch it!' said Rusty as the cushion thudded against the back of his head. 'I'm watching the Fluffy Fighter Show here.'

Tom smirked. Even though his brother Rusty was old enough to get his driver's licence, he still liked watching cartoons.

'Rusty, the cushion,' Tom said.

Rusty threw the pink flamingo over his head and it landed on Eddie's lap. Eddie was the book worm of the family and without even looking up from his latest action novel, he flung the flamingo across to Tom.

Tom puffed the cushion and tried to get comfortable. But he couldn't. Why did they have such lumpy couches AND lumpy cushions?

This time Tom gave the cushion an enormous thump. With a loud WHOOSH, it exploded. Thousands of tiny white feathers cannonballed across the lounge room.

The four brothers froze as it rained feathers on them. Tom had not been this surprised since the cat left a fur ball in his bike helmet.

The feathers floated in the air and landed on everything in sight. Feathers had even landed on the touch lamp, making the bulb flick on and off like a retro glitter ball.

Henry jumped up and danced a little jig. 'Oh yeah, now that's what I call a disco!'

Rusty laughed so hard a feather went up his nose, making him sneeze.

'Check this out!' said Eddie, as he used his book as a fan to see how long he could keep the feathers in the air.

'What's going on in there?' called Mum from the kitchen.

'Nothing, Mum,' Tom called back, trying to grab feathers. Every time he reached for one, it floated away in the opposite direction.

'What are we gonna do? That was Mum's favourite cushion,' said Henry, still dancing around the room. He didn't really seem too concerned.

The four brothers exchanged looks.

Suddenly Rusty jumped up. 'I've got an idea!'

He grabbed the vacuum from the nearby cupboard and began waving the hose around, sucking up feathers.

'What's going on now?' called Mum again.

'Just doing a little cleaning,' said Eddie. 'Don't come in, we were going to surprise you.' He gave Tom a wink. Tom had to cover his mouth to stifle giggles.

'Oh that's nice!' said Mum, her tone, all of a sudden, brighter.

Feathers flew frantically as Rusty waved the vacuum in every direction. Eddie used his book again to fan the feathers towards the vacuum, while Henry used his dance moves to push the feathers along.

When the feathers were finally cleared up, Henry grabbed the pink flamingo cushion cover and held it open, while Rusty grabbed handfuls of feathers from the vacuum bag and shoved them back in.

'There, good as new,' said Rusty as he tied the corner of the cushion in a knot and propped it once again under Tom's cast.

'Man, that thing sticks out like a chunky flagpole,' Henry said, poking Tom's leg.

'Does not!' said Tom.

'An enormously chunky flagpole,' Henry laughed. He picked up two stray feathers and stuck them in between Tom's toes. 'Every flagpole needs a flag.'

'Come on, quit fooling around. We'll be late for basketball practice,' said Eddie. 'See ya, Tom.'

The three older boys left.

Basketball. Just another thing I can't do for six weeks. Just great.

An hour later, the feathers were still wedged between Tom's toes because he couldn't reach them. They stared at him like a flag of surrender.

Tom wiggled his toes and the white flagged

waved. He frowned.

He was not going to give up. There were plenty of things he could do until his leg healed. He could play games on his DS whenever he wanted. What kid wouldn't like to do that?

But he'd already won all the races on Go Huffy Go, the coolest car racing game ever. And he'd scored all the goals on Giggle Soccer Across the Universe. And challenged all the characters in Wobble World.

Maybe he could watch television, or play board games?

Make that 'bored' games. They're what you play when you're bored, after all.

Tom whacked the lounge with his fist and the pink flamingo cushion catapulted across the room.

What was he going to do?

Chapter 2

'Hey, Tom, wanna play a DS game?' his friend, Howard, asked as he walked into the room. His messy hair fell across his eyes, which made his long, skinny emu legs trip over the rug. He landed on the flag of surrender. It waved excitedly.

'Ow!' Tom yelled at his friend. 'Get off me!'

'Sorry, Tom.' Howard untangled himself and plonked down on the floor. He took the feathers from Tom's toes and used them to blow his nose.

'Gross!' said Tom.

'Can I do anything to help?' Howard said.

'No, thanks,' Tom said. 'You might end up breaking my other leg.'

Howard looked down. 'I'm sorry. It was an accident.'

'I know it was!' Tom snapped.

Tom knew he should forgive Howard—he could see that his best friend was really sorry—but he just couldn't.

Two days ago at soccer training, Tom had kicked the ball towards the goal posts. Mud had flicked off his shin pads like little brown torpedoes as he began running after it, knowing a goal was in sight. However, Howard, thinking he could help, had also started running towards the ball. Howard's foot had gotten caught on a patch of weeds and he had tripped. He had fallen on Tom and they both had heard a loud snap: Tom's leg.

Tom clenched his teeth and looked away. This wasn't like the time Howard had bumped him into the pool fully-dressed, or sneezed on him with a mouthful of jelly. This was bigger. *Worse.*

'Can I get you an ice block or something?' Howard asked.

'Sure, whatever.'

Howard headed for the kitchen, this time stepping carefully around the rug. He put the soggy feathers in his pocket.

If only my leg wasn't broken. It was the worst thing that could have possibly happened.

No soccer for the rest of the season.

No tree climbing with Nelly, the girl next door.

No billy kart races down Chicken Hill.

Tom put his head in his hands and sighed. He could hear Howard rummaging through the freezer for the last blue-lime ice block. Tom groaned loudly, and then laughed at himself. He sounded like one of his brothers sitting on a whoopee cushion.

And then he stopped laughing. He suddenly remembered something.

Something HUGE.

Tom's muscles tightened. He held his breath.

How could he forget?

ADVENTURE WITH MY BROTHERS!

On Saturday, Eddie had something amazing planned, Henry had something awesome planned, and Rusty had something really cool planned.

Tom had been looking forward to this weekend longer than he could remember.

Tom exhaled like a whoopee cushion again. Would Mum let him go with his leg in a cast?

Probably not.

But I will not surrender.

Tom thought hard. Maybe there was a way he could still go. His heart beat a little faster as ideas swirled around his brain. He was thinking so hard that he barely heard the noise Howard was making.

In the kitchen, Howard had dropped a frozen lasagne on the floor. The lasagne bounced across the tiles and knocked open the dog flap. The dog flap opened just in time for Black Beauty, the little white bunny next door, to jump through.

'Come here, you critter!' yelled Howard as he chased the flying ball of fur. He took a leap and skidded across the tiles on his stomach, catching Black Beauty just before he hopped up the staircase.

Howard tucked Black Beauty into his shirt and then wedged the lasagne in the freezer.

By the time Howard returned to the lounge room with the ice blocks and a fidgety rabbit, Tom was smiling and rubbing his hands together. While Howard had been in the kitchen, he had come up with the perfect idea. Tom didn't have to miss out on adventure just because his leg was broken.

Chapter 3

Tom woke up Saturday morning and glanced out the window, squinting at the brightness.

This was going to be an awesome day. He could just feel it.

'Tom, close the curtains.' Henry groaned as he rolled over to face the wall.

'Sorry,' Tom whispered. He yanked the curtains closed, but knocked over his giant stuffed squirrel, the one Aunt Mavis gave him for his tenth birthday. It fell into Henry's spider tank.

Tom shuddered. He wasn't a fan of Henry's pet, Terry the Tarantula.

He pinched the squirrel by the ear and gently pulled it upwards, but Terry had already crawled onto the squirrel's big, fluffy tail.

'Get off,' Tom whispered to the spider, and even gave the squirrel a shake.

But Terry the Tarantula wouldn't budge. His hairy legs grabbed the squirrel even tighter.

Tom looked around for something to get the spider off. His book called *1001 Weird Things Every Kid Should Know* was just within reach, so he grabbed it and gently pushed the spider off the squirrel. The spider scurried onto the book, and Tom let go with a yelp.

Oh shoot, thought Tom.

Now the book and the squirrel were both in the tank. The book had landed open at Weird Thing No. 208: *the bird-eating spider has a leg span of 30 cm.*

Good thing Terry the Tarantula wasn't a bird-eating spider.

Tom grabbed his ruler and stuck a huge wad of Blu-Tack on the end of it. He retrieved the book and squirrel from the tank, before the spider decided they belonged to him now.

Finally, Tom snuck out of the bedroom and headed for the stairs. He'd worked up a sweat because of the spider. Now, with a cast on his leg, going down twenty-two steps meant twenty-two hops.

By the time Tom reached the last step, he was panting. But it was worth it. He was not going to be left behind. Tom was sure that one of his brothers would let him tag along today.

I will not surrender.

Tom hobbled towards the kitchen with a determined look on his face. He just knew he could convince Mum that his days of adventure were not over.

'Morning, Mum,' Tom said. Sunlight streamed through the kitchen windows. The smell of toast made his stomach rumble.

'You're up early,' Mum said.

Tom shrugged. 'Just want to get an early start, that's all.'

He sat on one chair and perched his broken leg on another. The plaster cast, which had been bright white two days ago, was now covered in scribble.

'Don't break a leg', Howard Butterfingers had written.

'Hop to it', Hannah Brown had written. Tom rolled his eyes at that one. 'Hope you like Chinese food', Ralphie Biggles had written. He'd said that Tom's leg looked like a king-size chopstick.

Tom grinned. A king-sized chopstick? He imagined himself karate chopping his way to the best adventure ever.

Chapter 4

'Henry was right, it does look like a chunky flagpole,' Eddie said as he stomped into the kitchen. He karate chopped Tom's arm.

'Hey, watch it,' Tom said. He reached out to hit Eddie back, but Eddie was already out of reach. Tom karate chopped the air instead.

Eddie laughed and then stepped closer so Tom could get him.

'Too bad you can't go ice skating,' Eddie said. 'How unlucky that you broke your leg.'

Eddie dropped bread into the toaster. His dark curly hair sprung out from his black beanie, bouncing with each step. It looked like a box jellyfish out of control.

Tom fidgeted in his chair and glanced at Mum.

He had never been ice skating in his life but knew it would be the most AMAZING thing in the world.

EVER.

Tom was going to launch his secret weapon—his amazing, incredible debating skills. His CHAMPION debating skills. He didn't win the debating team trophy last year for nothing. All he had to do was wait for just the right time.

No problem.

'Oh, man!' groaned Eddie as he tried to slap some butter on his toast, but most of it fell onto the kitchen bench. He then reached for the jam, attempting this time to get more on the toast than the bench.

But Tom was no longer watching Eddie—he was mesmerised by the yellow lump of butter on the bench as it slowly started to melt. It was like a watching a snowman on a tropical island—one minute it's there, the next minute it's a pool of liquid.

Eddie hadn't noticed the pool of liquid, so when he put the jam jar back on the bench, it glided right through the runny butter like a cross country skier and started hurtling towards the edge.

FAST.

Tom reached out to grab it but he was too late. The hurtling jam was about to topple over the edge. Tom had to do SOMETHING to stop the jar crashing to the ground and spewing jam all over the kitchen—being covered in sticky strawberry was definitely NOT on his list of things to do today. Thinking fast, he grabbed the loaf of bread in front of him and chucked it over the jam so it landed on the other side of the bench. Like a barricade, the bread stopped the skidding jam just in time.

Tom breathed a sigh of relief. Eddie looked up as the jam came to a halt. 'Good one,' he chuckled.

'Thanks,' said Tom.

Now was his chance. Tom looked at Mum, took a deep breath and announced that he was going ice skating.

'First, I can easily skate with a broken leg: Eddie can push me across the ice on a chair. I can even hang on to the side of the ice rink and push myself along,' said Tom. His argument was perfect. This was too easy.

'Second, I can just put one skate on,' he continued, 'and if I use my crutches, then I won't fall over.'

There was NO WAY Mum could argue with that.

'Nice try,' Mum said.

Tom raised his eyebrows. 'Come on, you know I've got really good balance.' He put his arms out as though he were walking a dangerous tightrope.

'Not a chance,' Mum said.

'But, Mum!'

'Nope. Forget it.'

Tom dropped his arms and almost fell off his chair. Did Mum really just say no? He was speechless. What was wrong with her? He really did have good balance, even with a broken leg.

Eddie shrugged and let Tom karate chop him on his way out. Tom did the best he could, but his heart wasn't in it. The chop wouldn't have ripped a sheet of tissue paper.

Tom watched Mum sip her coffee. He didn't understand why his debating skills had failed. He had once beaten Hannah Brown, and she was the best debater in the entire school.

Compared to her, Mum should be a knock over.

He was not about to give up. He still had two chances. In the end, he would triumph and get to have his adventure with one of his brothers. He took a gigantic bite of toast and munched away.

He could taste victory.

Chapter 5

Henry breezed in next and slapped Tom with a blue rubber flipper.

'Hey, watch it,' Tom grinned and reached for the flipper. He turned the flipper on its side like it was a shark circling its prey. Kind of like the way he was circling in on Mum.

Henry tried to dodge the shark but couldn't move very fast in his tight wetsuit. The swimming goggles perched on Henry's curly red hair looked like a surprised fluffy cat was sitting up there.

'Too bad you can't go water skiing,' Henry said. 'How unlucky you broke your leg.'

Tom had never been water skiing in his life (in fact, he had never even been on a boat). He thought it must be the most AWESOME thing in the world.

Tom threw the flipper aside and sat up. He knew just what he was going to say. There was no way Mum was going to say no *this time*.

Henry splashed juice all over the kitchen bench and the jar of jam started sliding again, heading for the other side of the bench. It bounced off the toaster, then the kettle, then the coffee machine. It was like a preserved fruit pinball machine. Tom reached out for the sliding jar but his arm wasn't long enough. The jam was like a steam train running out of track.

'Quick, the flipper!' Tom cried. Henry threw Tom the flipper, and he held it out. The jam skidded off the bench and landed safely on the flipper.

'Too cool,' said Henry.

'Thanks,' said Tom, handing him the jam. Henry put it back in the fridge.

Then Tom used his most confident voice and told Mum that water skiing with a broken leg was not a problem.

'First, I could just sit in the boat and steer. I could make sure everyone had a life jacket on. I could even hand out the sandwiches at lunch,' Tom said. 'I would be doing Henry a favour, really.'

Mum didn't say a word. Tom continued.

'Second, if I get a chance to water ski, I can just ski on a board,' he said. 'I can stick my leg out in front of me. I won't lose my balance and the cast won't get wet.'

Tom smiled sweetly as he spoke. He could almost taste the salt water.

Mum sipped her coffee again. 'Not a chance.'

'But Mum,' cried Tom, 'it will work, trust me. And in case I fall in, I can wrap the cast in plastic. It definitely won't get wet or soggy then.'

'We don't have that much cling wrap, Tom.'

'But Mum just listen—'

'Not gonna happen.'

Tom scowled. What was he doing wrong? It was as if Mum had superhuman will power to resist him. The cling wrap was a great idea. Why couldn't she see that?

Henry gave Tom a friendly pat on the shoulder as he left. Tom's stomach churned as he watched his brother waddle away. Mum was hard to crack but he still wasn't going to give up.

His heart raced.

He waited for Rusty. His last chance.

Chapter 6

When Rusty came into the kitchen, Tom raised his hand for a high-five. Rusty reached out to slap Tom's hand but at the last moment ruffled his hair.

'Hey, cut that out!' Tom laughed. He pulled Rusty's baseball cap down over his eyes.

'Good one.' Rusty laughed. He strode over to the fridge and his thick hiking boots squeaked loudly.

Tom watched his every move. He wasn't going to let this chance slip through his fingers.

'Too bad you can't go hiking, little brother,' Rusty said as he raided the fridge. 'Shame about your leg.'

Tom frowned at his chunky chopstick and wished it were gone. He had never been hiking in his life but thought it must be the COOLEST thing in the world.

Especially if Rusty was going.

Well, here goes nothing.

'It's good that I didn't go water skiing or ice skating,' Tom said calmly, 'hiking is much better with a broken leg. I'll be able to help Rusty heaps. I'll lay the crutches across two boulders and make a comfortable seat for everyone.'

Mum rolled her eyes.

Tom ignored it and kept going.

'Or I can go in the wheelchair and Rusty can push me along to cut a path through the bush. I won't even break out in a sweat.'

'Nice try,' Mum said.

Tom threw his toast aside. He just couldn't let this chance go.

'Mum, please, just listen. We could put mountain bike tyres on the wheelchair, and it would be a smooth ride.'

Mum sighed. 'Not even if you put on training wheels and a cute little bell.'

'But Mum,' Tom pleaded.

'Sorry, kiddo.'

'Not fair!' Tom growled.

'Hey Mum,' Rusty said, 'what if I promise to look out for him?'

Tom looked up hopefully but Mum just sighed. 'I'm sorry, boys. I want you to have some fun, Tom, I really do, but you can't go hiking with a broken leg. Maybe some other time.'

Tom just couldn't believe it. None of his arguments worked, not even when Rusty promised to look out for him. He slumped in his chair.

Were his days of adventure really over?

Chapter 7

'Why don't you do something with Howard?' Rusty suggested.

'No way,' snapped Tom. 'He broke my leg.'

'That's true,' Rusty said. 'But he's still you friend. Just think about it.'

He patted Tom on the back and left to go hiking.

Tom wasn't very hungry now. He played with his toast, tearing the crusts off and lining them up like bones on an archaeological dig. Jabba the Mutt bounded through their dog flap and jumped up onto the kitchen table. Tom yelped with surprise as Jabba the Mutt's little paws skidded in juice and he lost his balance. The dog landed on his round belly, and skidded off the table just as Dad walked into the kitchen. Without blinking an eye, Dad caught Jabba the Mutt mid-air and put him under his arm.

'What's up, sport?' Dad asked as Jabba the Mutt squirmed happily, 'Anything exciting planned for today?'

Tom sighed. 'Nope. Nothing at all.'

'Don't be silly,' Mum said, 'we're going shopping this morning and we're going to have a great time. There's a sale on at Dingles Department Store.'

'Shopping!' Tom moaned in dismay. 'Oh, Dad, you've got to let me stay home with you. Please?'

There was nothing worse than a shopping trip with Mum, except maybe helping Dad trim Grandpa's nose hairs. That always grossed him out.

Dad put Jabba the Mutt on the floor and gave him a pat. 'Sorry, kiddo, but I promised Grandpa I'd mow the old nose lawn for him.'

Tom rolled his eyes. It seemed he was going shopping after all, and that wasn't very adventurous.

If it was anything like last time, it might be embarrassing, especially if Mum had anything to do with it.

Chapter 8

Tom sunk deep into the chair and lowered his baseball cap. He kept his eyes on the ground and tried to ignore the people that walked past him.

Some adventure.

Tom hoped that no one recognised him in the wheelchair. It was his grandmother's old chair, and it had been sitting in the garage for years. The chair creaked when the wheels rolled and the bolts were so loose that it wobbled even when it was standing still.

How far will we get before one of the wheels falls off this thing?

Tom shifted in the seat and tried to get comfortable, but it was impossible. His broken leg was propped up so it stuck straight out in front of him. The seat had a large tear in it and bits of foam poked out. It kind of looked like a volcano of cheese; it ponged like dried-up rotten eggs.

Every time Tom moved, more foam oozed out. *IT STUNK!*

'Seriously, Mum, do we have to use the wheelchair?' Tom wrinkled his nose and wished for his crutches. But they were at home in the cupboard because Mum said he was too slow with them.

'Yes we do. Now let's get a move on,' Mum said, pushing him along.

Tom gripped the chair. His body stiffened, making more smelly foam escape. He held his breath until the smell passed.

He just never knew what was going to happen when Mum pushed. Sometimes she pushed fast, and other times slow. Lots of times she ran the chair into things and didn't even notice.

Like now. Tom was so busy trying to stop the foam erupting that he didn't see it until it was too late.

'Mum, look out!' Tom cried as the wheelchair rammed into a shopping trolley.

Groceries went everywhere.

A bag of lemons flew into the air. Tom instantly reached up to grab them, but instead poked a hole in the bag.

'Oh crikey!' he yelled.

The lemons hit the ground like jumbo hail and bounced towards the fish stall. They crashed into the stall with a huge BANG. King prawns were hurled across the shopping centre.

Without thinking, Tom lunged forward and caught the soaring crustaceans one at a time. He'd never moved so fast in his life.

'That was AWESOME!' the fish stall owner said, and the little crowd of people nearby clapped. Tom beamed as he handed back the prawns.

'No problem,' Tom said. It *had* been kind of awesome.

Then, out of nowhere, a packet of frozen peas slapped him in the back of the head. Tom looked around and saw a lady holding the trolley he had run into. She was glaring at him and shaking a bony fist.

'Watch where you're going, young man!'

'Sorry, but it wasn't my fault,' Tom said, before she could throw anything else at him. He tossed the peas back into her trolley.

'And what about my lemons?' she asked. Her grey hair bun wobbled frantically.

'I can help you pick them up, if you like?' Tom offered, but she waved him off.

Tom shrugged and leaned back in the chair, making the cheese volcano erupt. In the excitement of prawn-catching, (which should be a national sport in his opinion), he had forgotten about the cheese volcano. His face went bright red and a moment later his eyes were watering. He sneaked a quick look at the lady. Her eyes were watering too.

'What is that awful smell?' She glanced around with alarm and then hurried away before Tom could answer.

Chapter 9

'Mum, hurry up!' Tom yelled.

'Okay, okay,' Mum said as she eyeballed a pair of fluffy green slippers.

Tom gripped the chair as the wheels rolled again. Every muscle in his body tensed. Would they ever get to Dingles? And would he get there in one piece?

Why couldn't I be with one of my brothers, right now? I would have probably been safer with them.

'Oh look who's over there,' Mum said with delight. The wheelchair abruptly skidded as Mum changed direction.

Mrs Biggles, one of Mum's gossipy friends, was sipping tea in a café, waving them over. Tom groaned and bounced in the chair. The cheese volcano spluttered. Mum sped up and they approached Mrs Biggles with alarming speed.

'Mum look out!' Tom said.

The wheelchair bumped into a nearby table. Tom's jaw dropped as the table pushed over a chair, which knocked over the specials blackboard, which flipped a basket of smiley-faced cupcakes into the air.

I can catch them, just like I caught the prawns, Tom thought to himself, but then realised there was no way he would get to them in time.

There were too many people in the way. The cupcakes were going to land at the other side of the café where a businessman was working on his laptop.

Tom watched the cupcakes smear across the ceiling of the café.

He had to think fast!

And then he saw the stack of plates. He quickly grabbed one and chucked it like a Frisbee. The plate spun through the air. As the cupcakes started falling, they landed on the spinning plate.

Before the plate hit the wall, a lady reached up and caught it.

'Got it! Wow, that was AMAZING!' said the lady with the great Frisbee skills. She put the plate of cakes on the counter as all the tea drinkers in the café applauded.

'You're welcome,' Tom said. It *was* kind of amazing.

Tom was getting ready to high-five the lady but froze mid-air.

Something was very wrong. And wet.

He looked down and saw a milkshake had spilt into his lap.

'Oh man!' Tom cried. What a waste of a perfectly good chocolate drink. Worse, he watched in horror as a big dark patch spread cross his pants.

I'm stuck in a wheelchair, looking like I didn't make it to the bathroom in time. Just great.

'Look at what you've done!' the café owner cried, 'there's milk everywhere!'

'I'm really sorry,' Tom said. He looked around at Mum, hoping she would help, but she was too busy chatting to Mrs Biggles. And when Mum got chatting, she didn't notice much of anything else.

Tom tried to help the café owner, but she waved him away. She mopped up the milk frantically.

Tom shrugged and grabbed some napkins to dry his pants. The napkins went mushy and his pants remained damp. Worst of all, the milk seeped into the rip in the chair and now the cheese volcano squelched loudly.

The awful smell now had an awful sound.

Mrs Biggles stared at Tom. He had a horrible feeling that she had heard the loud squelch and that the cheesy volcano smell had wafted past her. Tom hoped she was too polite to say anything.

He had to get Mum moving.

'Mum … um … don't we have to get to Dingles? There's a sale, remember, and I'd hate for you to miss out.'

'Okay, okay, I didn't realise you were so keen,' Mum said.

'If only you knew,' Tom muttered.

As they left the café, Mum frowned. 'Why on earth would they sell cupcakes like that?' she said.

Tom looked at the cupcakes and giggled. The smiley faces now looked like something out of Frankenstein.

As they headed towards Dingles, the wheelchair left a milky trail behind. It looked like railway tracks on a crazy rollercoaster ride.

'Oh just look at that,' Mum shrieked as she let go of the wheelchair a third time. In the next moment she grabbed handfuls of earrings from a jewellery shop.

'You've got to be kidding me!' Tom said as the chair bounded towards a discount shop.

Tom tightened his grip. The turning wheels burned the palms of his hands.

Piles of toothpaste, sunglasses and pool toys were getting closer ... and closer.

So was an old man, who was looking at dental floss.

'Look out!' Tom cried.

Tom missed the man just in time, but the wheelchair bounced over two bumps before colliding with a stack of bubble bath bottles.

Tom looked around, confused.

What had just happened?

Chapter 10

'Oowww!' the man cried. He threw down the floss and clutched one foot, and then the other, hopping in circles.

The wheelchair had run over his brown leather shoes as if they had been puny speed humps.

'Watch out, kid!' the man said.

'I'm so sorry. I tried to miss you.'

And that was when Tom saw something out of the corner of his eye. A bottle of bubble bath at the top of the pile had begun to wobble.

It was going to land on a nearby baby's pram. Tom just had to get that bottle of bubble bath before it fell.

He looked around and saw a giant inflatable dolphin dangling from a fishing rod nearby. He grabbed the rod and swung the dolphin as hard as he could, knocking the bubble bath off course.

The bottle shook and flipped, spinning higher and higher.

Then the lid popped off and hundreds of bubbles sprung into the air. The bottle landed on the ground, away from the pram.

The toddler in the pram squealed with glee, grasping at the bubbles that floated near her.

'Nice job, dolphin boy,' said the girl at the checkout. 'That was the COOLEST thing.'

'Thanks!' said Tom, grinning. It *was* kind of cool.

Tom put his hands behind his head and was leaning back to enjoy the flying bubble show when suddenly, the cheese volcano echoed loudly throughout the shopping centre.

Tom's face reddened. Then his eyes watered again as the smell hung around like a thick fog. Nearby shoppers stopped in their tracks and looked about, trying to figure out where it was coming from.

If I just act normal, no one will think it's coming from the wheelchair.

Tom looked around as though he didn't know where the smell was coming from. The girl at the checkout glanced at him and he shrugged innocently, as if to say, *Hey, I don't know either.* When she looked away, Tom breathed out loudly.

That was close.

'My pinkie toe hurts,' said the hopping man with the squished toes. Thankfully, he didn't seem to notice the sound or smell.

'Again, mister, I'm really sorry,' Tom said to the man.

The man waved him off and hopped away, changing feet every couple of hops.

Tom frowned. Three times he had said sorry for things that weren't his fault and three times no one had believed him.

They wouldn't accept my apology.

A familiar, guilty feeling was swirling in his gut.

But hang on a minute—I didn't accept Howard's apology, either, when he offered it. Is this what he feels like?

Tom rubbed his eyes. His head hurt as though

he'd been whacked with a bag of hard-boiled lollies. Or frozen peas.

Tom and Howard had not had any fun together since the broken leg. There had been no giggles, even though Howard had tripped over lots of things since then. And there had been no Giggle Soccer Across the Universe challenges or games of Spot the Blob.

Things just weren't the same.

Is it because I won't forgive him?

Chapter 11

'Yap! Yap! Yap! Yap!'

Tom whipped his head around to see where the sound was coming from. The high-pitched noise hurt his ear drums. Tom glanced around at the shop windows, half expecting them to shatter.

The noise was getting closer.

'What now?' Tom muttered.

And then he saw the little brown and white dog with a black spot on its cheek. The dog's stumpy, little tail whipped around in circles like a helicopter propeller.

The dog was on the loose.

It pounced across the shopping centre with its lead dragging behind. Its mouth was wide open and its tongue flapped across the side of its cheek, bouncing up and down with each pounce.

The dog looked as though he were running through a field of grass instead of a maze of people and trolleys.

'Flapjack! Come back!'

In the distance, Tom saw the dog's owner. Her long blue dress shimmered as she took fast, dainty steps. The CLINK CLINK CLINK of her high-heeled shoes sounded like tap dancing at double speed.

The lady was not moving very fast. Tom couldn't help giggling. She looked like one of those cartoon characters running on the spot but getting nowhere. Like when the cat was being chased by a ninja on the Fluffy Fighter show this morning.

She's never going to catch that dog, Tom thought as the dog headed right towards him. 'But maybe I can.'

He didn't think the dog was going to jump onto his lap, but would probably run right past him. But maybe, just maybe, he could grab the lead as the dog sprinted by.

As the dog got closer, Tom focused on the lead whipping around. It would hit the ground, and then flick up into the air before falling to the ground again.

The next time the lead flicked up, Tom was going to catch it. He held his breath and waited for just the right moment.

When Flapjack got close, Tom lunged for the lead. The soggy foam complained loudly, but he didn't hear it or smell it. Dog slobber sprayed him like a sun shower. He didn't care.

The only thing he saw at that moment was the lead. His fingers touched it. It was within his reach … but they tightened over thin air.

'Missed it!' Tom slapped the arm of the wheelchair.

And then, almost instantly, the wheelchair started moving.

FAST.

Tom looked back, expecting to see Mum pushing it, but she wasn't there. She was still looking at earrings.

How was he moving? The wheelchair suddenly yanked to the right.

Tom looked around and then he saw it …

Chapter 12

Tom's eyes widened as he drew a sharp breath. 'You've got to be kidding me!'

The dog's lead was caught on his cast.

He tried to untangle the lead from his foot but it was impossible. It was the flag of surrender all over again.

The wheelchair rolled faster and faster. Tom felt as though he was in a sled being pulled by a husky. Crowds of people leapt out of the way as the dog pulled Tom along.

How on earth was he going to get out of this mess?

'Mum! Help!' Tom glanced over his shoulder. But Mum was at the checkout paying for her new earrings.

It was up to him.

'Pancake! Or Flapjack; whatever your name is. STOP!'

But the dog's stumpy legs sped up. The chair was yanked along, barely missing a stand full of wigs.

Tom tried to grip the wheels, but the tyres burned his hands and left black tread marks across his palms. His hands smelled like rubber, but the chair didn't slow down.

They sped past a toy store, around a bouncy castle full of squealing kids, and dodged a fruit stall.

This dog is worse than Mum!

His baseball cap flicked off his head and landed on a juicy round melon. Tom didn't care. He didn't even notice the smell of popcorn as they rolled past the cinema.

'Yap! Yap! Yap!' the dog barked merrily as Tom bumped a man carrying a box of marbles. The marbles hit the floor and rolled everywhere.

Tom watched as people lost their balance and flayed their arms about, trying to keep from falling over. It looked as if they were doing some kind of Mexican fast dance.

And still the dog ran.

'Whoa, boy!' Sweat flew off Tom's forehead as the dog took a sharp corner. The right wheel lifted into the air for a moment and then slammed down hard. The cheese volcano thundered and yellow foam splattered across the dress of a lady carrying a pie. The lady shrieked and threw her arms into the air. The pie went flying. It went:

past a man (who jumped out of the way);

over a girl's head (she tried to reach for it but missed);

into a pet shop (where there was a duck that ducked just in time)

and splattered on a parrot's beak. The bird squawked as pastry burst like a crusty fireworks display. Apple chunks were glued to soft red feathers, until the parrot realised that apple pie was actually very tasty.

What a waste of pie.

Then, out of nowhere, an idea of how to stop the dog popped into Tom's head.

Tom grinned as he stared at the hotdog stand up ahead.

Chapter 13

The smell of hotdogs made Tom's mouth water.

The hotdog man was arranging sauce bottles along the front of the stand. His shirt stretched tightly across his large stomach and the buttons strained with every movement.

'Yap! Yap! Yap! Yap!'

The hotdog man looked up so quickly that Tom expected the man's buttons to pop off and knock over the sauce bottles.

'Please may I have a hotdog?' Tom shouted as they got closer.

The man nodded. As Tom sailed by, he reached out and the man passed him the hotdog like a baton in a relay race.

The soft bun squished in Tom's hand. He was

tempted to take a bite—a big juicy bite—but stopped himself just in time. The hotdog wasn't for him.

It was for Flapjack.

Tom lurched forward and held out the hotdog. Sauce dripped through his fingers and ran down the side of the cast.

'Here boy!' he called. 'Dinner!'

The dog's ears twitched and the stumpy legs froze. The wheelchair skidded to a halt and almost threw Tom to the floor, but he stopped himself from falling just in time. The dog put his nose in the air and sniffed.

'Come and get it, boy!' Tom waved the hotdog and used his good leg to anchor himself. This time he was prepared.

The dog ate the sausage and bun right out of Tom's hand. Tom grabbed the collar and held tight as the dog licked the sauce from his fingers.

He threw his head back and laughed. He had dog slobber on his hands but it was the most fun he'd ever had.

Flapjack's owner tap danced her way over to Tom. She untangled the lead and picked up the dog. Dog slobber oozed down her dress.

'Thank you, young man,' she said with delight.

'Thank you for being so very brave.'

'Aw, it's nothing,' Tom said.

He was glad he had finally stopped the dog, but skidding in the wheelchair had been the best of all. Even with the cheese volcano.

Especially with the cheese volcano.

He couldn't wait to show Howard. He could picture Howard's hearty laugh, getting Tom to do it again and again. Tom also knew that Howard would want to try it but, instead of skidding, he would probably end up flat on the ground with the wheelchair on top of him.

Howard would do it all wrong but it wouldn't matter. They'd chuckle about it for days.

For the first time since his leg broke, Tom really missed his best friend.

Tom knew what he had to do.

'Well,' the lady said, 'I still think you deserve a reward for saving my Flapjack.'

'Really?' Tom watched as she juggled Flapjack in one hand and dug into her neat little handbag with the other. He sat up eagerly. It wasn't every day he got a reward of … five dollars? Maybe even ten dollars? That would buy some lolly bananas for him and Howard.

The lady pulled out a crisp $100 note and gave it to Tom.

Tom's eyes widened. He held up the money and stared at it. He had never had $100 before in his life. 'Wow! Thank you!'

But the lady was already tap dancing away. Flapjack yapped and licked her cheek as she cuddled him.

Tom couldn't wait to tell Howard.

Chapter 14

Tom balanced himself on the lounge, straining to look out the window. Nelly's cat scurried across the street, its grey fur puffed up like a fluffy blowfish. Jabba the Mutt barked—not a *Yap! Yap! Yap!* but a real bark—as he rolled in the grass.

Then, Tom saw Howard walking up the street. Howard was so busy watching the cat that he walked into a tree. Tom laughed and opened the window.

'Howard! Come on in.'

Howard waved and jogged across the street. Within a minute he was in the room. He tried not to look at the plaster cast covered in scribbles, drawings and hotdog sauce.

'Howard, I'm sorry for acting like such a goof,'

Tom said, making room for his best friend. 'I know you didn't mean to break my leg.'

Howard sat down with a sigh of relief. 'Thanks, Tom. I felt really awful about it. What made you change your mind?'

'Let's just say I had some sense *knocked* into me. Literally. It's time to get on with being friends again.' Tom grabbed Howard and put him in a headlock. Howard quickly got out and tried to put Tom in a headlock. He bumped his knee on the coffee table.

'Good one.' Tom laughed.

Howard rubbed his sore knee, but was soon laughing with him. It was a real, hearty belly laugh. Tom finally understood what it meant to forgive. Things were back to normal again.

'So what do you want to do now?' Howard asked.

'For starters, help me think of a way to spend this.' Tom held up the $100 note.

Howard fell off the lounge.

The boys were still deciding what to do with the money when Eddie limped into the room. His jeans were soaking wet and ripped at the knees.

The box jellyfish on his head now looked like fried seaweed.

'You're lucky you didn't go ice skating,' Eddie groaned. 'It was awful. The power went out and all the ice melted. We got washed down the street and now I've got grazes all over my legs.'

'No ice skating? Well, let me tell you about my day,' Tom said eagerly. 'Something AMAZING happened.'

'I'm sure it was really amazing at Dingles,' Eddie said. 'Tell me later.' He limped towards the stairs.

Tom and Howard looked at each other and shrugged. Maybe Henry or Rusty would listen.

Chapter 15

Henry waddled in cradling a pair of broken blue rubber flippers. His mouth drooped and his hair stood on end.

'You're lucky you didn't go water skiing,' Henry sighed. 'It was terrible. The boat sank and we had to swim back to shore. It took hours.'

'No water skiing? Well something *AWESOME* happened to me today.'

'You can tell me all about your awesome new t-shirt later,' Henry said as he dragged himself to the stairs. Tom and Howard smiled at each other. No ice skating *or* water skiing?

Soon Rusty hobbled in. He took slow, wide steps like a cowboy ready for a showdown. Tom raised his eyebrows and stared at his brother.

'You're lucky you didn't go hiking,' Rusty groaned. 'It was gross. I squatted to go to the loo and ended up on a patch of poison ivy. Ooowwww!'

Tom put his hands over his mouth to smother a laugh. No wonder he was walking funny. He didn't dare look at Howard. One look and he wouldn't be able to hold the giggles in.

When the urge to laugh had passed, Tom said, 'A patch of ivy?'

'You'd better believe it,' Rusty said. 'I won't be able to sit down for a week.'

Tom grinned. 'I've just got to tell you what happened to me today. It was really COOL.'

'It really was,' Howard said, 'You should hear it.'

'I'm sure shopping with Mum was really cool. Tell me after I've had a shower,' Rusty said.

Tom almost sprung out of his seat. 'But Howard and I are friends again.'

Rusty gave Tom a hearty high-five. Then they both gave Howard a high-five.

Rusty headed for the stairs. Tom remembered the $100 note. His eyes brightened. 'You won't believe what else happened!'

'Can't wait to hear it,' Rusty said. 'Just give me a minute.'

Rusty hobbled away, scratching his pants as if they were full of fleas. Tom and Howard looked at each other and the giggles escaped after all.

Tom began to think he wasn't so unlucky after all. Sure, he had missed out on going ice skating, water skiing and hiking all because of a broken leg.

But, he had had the most AMAZING, AWESOME, COOLEST day ever, for the same reason. And he had his best friend back, which was the best of all.

And I did not surrender.

Not when he juggled prawns and caught cupcakes or flung a dolphin; not when he had a rollercoaster ride on a cheese volcano or in a dog sled going through a crazy maze. Things hadn't turned out the way he wanted, but something even better had happened. Tom chuckled.

It was like a great adventure swap, just when he least expected it.

Later that day, Mum drove Tom and Howard to the shops. Tom couldn't wait to spend the money. Best of all, Mum let him use the crutches while Howard gave the wheelchair a try. He drove over every bump he could find to make the cheese volcano erupt.

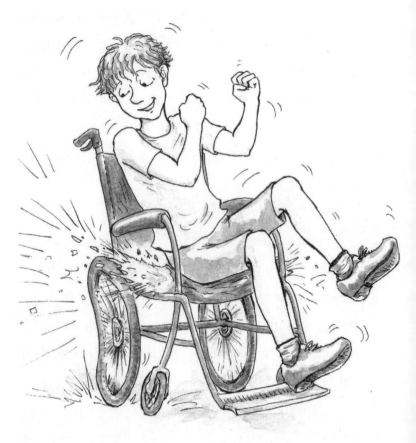

Tom bought the latest Wobble World DS game, the one that gave you jelly throwing superpowers, and spent the rest of the money on sour worms. He shared them with his best friend Howard but also saved some for his brothers, especially after the day they'd had. The lollies made their tongues tingle, and they made the funniest sour faces ever. Tom laughed so hard that tears squirted from his watery-green eyes.

Tom's days of adventure weren't over, after all. In fact, they were better than ever!

Meet Lisa Limbrick

Lisa Limbrick lives in NSW with her husband and two children. She enjoys many extreme sports such as knitting and gardening. She has always loved writing and began writing children's stories several years ago when her family decided to drive across Australia and back. She especially loves writing stories which are full of humour, oddities and everything in between!

Lisa completed a PhD in education, where she focused on reading interventions and reading progress for primary school children. She has a passion for encouraging children not only to read well, but to love reading. Her children's books are full of bright, colourful imagery, designed to capture the imagination of the most reluctant reader.

Meet Jemima Trappel

Jemima is a Sydney-based artist and illustrator who enjoys riding her bicycle. Like many illustrators she was born holding a pencil and uses it frequently to bring words to life.

She decided to make a career out of her passion, and in 2012, after five years at the College of Fine Arts and the University of NSW, she emerged with a Bachelor of Fine Arts (with honours), a Bachelor of Arts (a combined degree) and the ability to converse in French.

Same by Katrina Roe, is her first book with Wombat Books. Prior to this, Jemima illustrated Wonderfully Madison (2013 – winner of the children's book category in the Caleb awards that year) and Fearlessly Madison (2014) by Penny Reeve (published by Youthworks Media). She is also the illustrator of the short comic, A friend in need, by Karen Bielharz (part of the self-published Kinds of Blue anthology, 2011), and is the linework artist for the short animation Money Tree (2011), written and directed by Hawanatu Bangura.